5 Ingredients 15 Minutes Prep Time Slow Cooker Cookbook: Quick & Easy Set It & Forget It Recipes

By Maria Holmes

All Rights Reserved. No part of this publication may be reproduced in any form or by any means, including scanning, photocopying, or otherwise without prior written permission of the copyright holder.
Copyright © 2013

All information in this book has been carefully researched and checked for factual accuracy. However, the author and publisher make no warranty, express or implied, that the information contained herein is appropriate for every individual, situation or purpose, and assume no responsibility for errors or omissions. The reader assumes the risk and full responsibility for all actions, and the authors will not be held responsible for any loss or damage, whether consequential, incidental, special or otherwise that may result from the information presented in this publication.

The author has relied on her own experience as well as many different sources for this book, and has done her best to check the facts and to give credit where it is due. In the event that any material is incorrect or has been used without proper permission, please contact the author so that the oversight can be corrected at:
HolmesCookedMeals@gmail.com

Table of Contents

Preface 1
Acknowledgement 3
Introduction 4
Slow Cooker Savvy 6
Crockery Conversions 7
Beef 8
Chicken 23
Fish 42
Pork 45
Turkey 57
Vegetarian 61
Conclusion 68
Index 70

Preface

Dear Reader!

I would like to take this opportunity to thank you for taking the time to read my book and hope that you find these "quick prep" slow cooker recipes interesting and tasty!

Before we start exploring how you can prepare great meals with as little as 5 ingredients and/or 15 minutes (or less) of prep work, I would like to introduce myself. My name is Maria Holmes and I am indeed the author of this slow cooker recipe book that you are now reading. If you are interested in learning more about me, my mission and my passion, please join my Facebook community at ***Homes Cooked Meals*** for interesting activities and enthusiastic discussions. Or you might want to visit my blog at www.holmescookedmeals.com.

But let's get back to the topic at hand - *5 Ingredients 15 Minutes Prep Time Slow Cooker Cookbook: Quick & Easy Set It & Forget It Recipes*.

I use my slow cooker all the time. Rarely does a week go by without using it at least once or twice. It allows me to simply put some ingredients in the slow cooker in the morning before going to work. Then when I come home, I am ready to enjoy a great dinner with my family. And what's even more amazing about a slow cooker is how easy it is to create a truly tasty meal with minimal ingredients. In fact, I often try to come up with great slow cooker meals that require only five ingredients. Keeping the list of ingredients this short means that it only takes a few minutes to pull the slow cooker out of the cupboard, toss in the ingredients, turn it on "LOW" and leave for the day, only to come home to an amazing home cooked meal.

In this cookbook, you will discover how easy it is to come home to (or wake up to) a delicious home-cooked meal that only requires 5 ingredients and/or 15 minutes (or less) of prep time.

So get ready to discover all the tasty simmered-in flavors of slow cooking.

Enjoy and be well!

Maria Holmes

Acknowledgement

I would like to express my gratitude to my parents, who have always supported and encouraged me in everything I have done in my life. Without their love and support, this book might never have been written.

I am also grateful to my dear friends who I often use as test subjects when developing my recipes. Without their help and sacrifice, many of these recipes may have turned out bland and tasteless. Many of these friends have become members and supporters of my Facebook Page and www.holmescookedmeals.com website.

And a special thank you goes out to my loving husband and my two amazing children (Ellie an Isaac) who endlessly encourage me to share my love for food and my many recipes with the world.

And most importantly, thank you, dear reader, for purchasing *5 Ingredients 15 Minutes Prep Time Slow Cooker Cookbook: Quick & Easy Set It & Forget It Recipes*.

Introduction

Fast Prep, Slow Cooking Meals

It's no coincidence that slow cookers are making a big comeback now, when people are busier than ever. These fast prep recipes were created for you: Someone who's moving at the speed of light, craves a comforting home-cooked meal, and doesn't want to spend his or her life in the kitchen. Each of these recipes requires 15 minutes or less of prep time and absolutely no acrobatics. If you can chop an onion and twist a can opener, you can make these dishes. The recipes include nutrition data, and most include serving tips.

No time to cook? No problem. All you need is 15 minutes of prep time, 5 ingredients (plus a few staples), and 1 turn of a switch, and you're set for dinner. Your slow cooker takes quick and easy meals to a whole new level.

Time Saving Tricks

If your kitchen time is always crunched, here are a few simple ways to ease the rush.

Plan Ahead: Take the time to create a weekly menu. Before you shop, be sure to read each recipe you plan to make to avoid extra trips to the grocery store.

Convenience Counts: Take advantage of convenience products. Chopped fresh and frozen vegetables, canned beans, and precut meats are just a few of the valuable time-saving products available.

Enlist Help: Ask the kids to help with easy prep work, clean-up, and setting the table.

Keep It Clean: A tidy kitchen is much easier to cook in than a messy one. Take a few minutes each day to clear clutter and straighten up.

Soak It Up

Many slow cooked foods are best served with a side dish that will absorb all its delicious juices. Stock up on these quick-to-make options and dinner will come together easier than ever.

Rice: Precooked long grain, whole grain, or brown rice is available in microwavable packets that heat up in under 2 minutes.

Couscous: This granular semolina tastes like pasta but cooks in a mere 5 minutes.

Mashed Potatoes: Look for prepared mashed potatoes in your supermarket's refrigerated section. They take just 5 minutes in the microwave.

Slow Cooker Savvy

Your slow cooker just may be the best kitchen helper you've ever had. Use these tips to get the most out of this resourceful appliance.

Herbs = Flavor: Herbs - both fresh and dried - enhance the flavor of food like nothing else. Add fresh herbs at the end of cooking so they retain their bright flavor. Add dried herbs earlier in the cooking process so their flavors have time to intensify and blend with other ingredients. Fresh and dried herbs can be used interchangeably: 1 teaspoon dried herbs equals 1 tablespoon fresh herb.

Don't Peek: As tempting as it may be to check the progress of dinner, don't lift the lid while your slow cooker is at work. Every time you lift the lid, heat is released and you'll need an additional 30 minutes of cooking time.

Vegetable Know-How: Dense vegetables, such as carrots, potatoes, and parsnips, are ideal for long, slow cooking. Add tender veggies, such as green beans, at the end of cooking. Cook according to recipe directions or on the high-heat setting for 30 minutes or until they are tender.

Thaw It First: Even if you're in a rush, never put frozen raw poultry or meat into the slow cooker. Because of the slow rate of cooking, frozen meat will hover in the food safety danger zone (40°F to 140°F) far too long.

Put It To The Test: Use this test to be sure your slow cooker is safe to use: Fill it half to two-thirds full with water. Heat it on the low-heat setting, covered, for 8 hours, then check the water temperature with a food thermometer. It should register 185°F. If not, it's time for a new slow cooker.

Crockery Conversions

Can favorite soups, stews, and roasts be adapted for the slow cooker? Absolutely! Here's how to do it.

Veggies: Cut vegetables into uniform pieces so they'll cook evenly and completely. Veggies take longer to cook than meat and poultry, so be sure to place them close to the heat, either around the sides of the slow cooker or at the bottom under the meat or poultry and liquid.

Liquids: Because the liquid doesn't boil away as it would with conventional cooking, you won't need as much for slow cooking. Whether your recipe calls for broth, wine, or water, reduce the liquid in the original recipe by about half.

Meat And Poultry: Select a recipe that uses a less-tender cut of meat, such as pork shoulder or beef chuck. Slow, moist cooking will soften the meat fibers and make these tougher cuts tender and juicy. If your roast is more than 2-1/2 pounds, cut it in half so it cooks evenly. Remove skin from poultry pieces. If desired, brown the meat or poultry in a skillet before adding it to the slow cooker.

Beans: To use beans that are dried instead of canned, you will need to precook them. Rinse the beans and place them in a saucepan then add enough water to cover the beans by 2 inches. Bring to boiling then reduce the heat. Let simmer, uncovered for 10 minutes then remove from heat. Cover and let stand for 1 hour. Drain and rinse th beans before adding them to the slow cooker.

Beef

THE RECIPES

Roast Beef with Mixed Fruit and Chipotle Sauce 9
Roast Beef Sandwich 11
Beef with Ancho Chile Stew..12
Corned Beef and Cabbage 13
Easy Taco Chili Stew...15
Italian-Style Meatballs with Basil Pesto Stew....................................16
Perfect Pot Roast 17
Beef and Marinara Sauce Stuffed Peppers 19
Swedish Meatballs with Ground Beef and Pork 21

Roast Beef with Mixed Fruit and Chipotle Sauce

Preparation time: 15 minutes
Cooking time: 10 to 11 hours (LOW) or 5 to 5-1/2 hours (HIGH)

Ingredients

1 3-pound boneless beef chuck pot roast
2 teaspoons garlic-pepper seasoning
1 package (7-ounces) dried mixed fruit
1/2 cup water
1 tablespoon finely chopped chipotle pepper in adobo sauce
2 teaspoons cornstarch
1 tablespoon cold water
Fresh cilantro sprigs (optional)

Directions

Trim the fat from the boneless beef chuck. If necessary, cut the beef chuck to fit into a 3-1/2 to 4-quart slow cooker. Sprinkle both sides of the beef chuck with the garlic pepper seasoning. Place the beef chuck in the slow cooker and add the dried fruit, the 1/2 cup water. and chipotle pepper.

Cover and cook on LOW for 10 to 11 hours of on HIGH for 5 to 5-1/2 hours.

Transfer the beef chuck and fruit to a serving dish and thinly slice the meat. Cover the meat and fruit to keep warm.

For the sauce, pour the cooking liquid into a bowl or a glass measuring cup and skim off the fat. Combine the cornstarch and the 1 tablespoon of cold water in a medium saucepan and stir in the cooking liquid. Cook and stir over medium heat until the mixture starts to thicken. Cook and stir for 2 minutes more.

Serve the meat and fruit with the sauce. If desired, garnish the meal with cilantro.

Makes 8 servings.

<u>Per Serving</u>

Calories: 275; Fat: 6g; Cholesterol: 101mg; Sodium: 378mg; Carbohydrate: 17g; Fiber: 1g; Protein: 37g

Roast Beef Sandwich

Pile melt-in-your-mouth beef onto whole-grain rolls for an extra fiber boost.

Preparation time: 15 minutes
Cooking time: 11 to 12 hours (LOW) or 5-1/2 to 6 hours (HIGH)

Ingredients

2 pounds boneless beef roast
3 medium onions, chopped
2 cups red wine vinegar
3 bay leaves
1/2 teaspoon garlic powder
1/2 teaspoon salt (optional)
1/4 teaspoon ground cloves

Directions

Cut the roast in half and place in a 4-quart or larger slow cooker.

Combine the onions, vinegar, bay leaves, garlic powder, salt (if using), and ground cloves and pour over the roast.

Cover and cook on LOW for 11 to 12 hours or on HIGH for 5-1/2 to 6 hours.

Discard the bay leaves and remove the meat from the slow cooker.

Shred the beef roast with 2 forks.

Makes 12 servings.

Per Serving

Calories: 230; Fat: 6g; Cholesterol: 45mg; Sodium: 630mg;
Carbohydrate: 27g; Fiber: 4g; Protein: 19g

Beef with Ancho Chile Stew

Bake some corn bread to go along with this chunky stew.

Preparation time: 15 minutes
Cooking time: 8 to 9 hours (LOW) or 4 to 4 1/2 hours (HIGH)

Ingredients

1 pound of boneless beef chuck roast
1 tablespoon ground ancho chile pepper
Nonstick cooking spray
1 package (16-ounces) frozen stew vegetables
1 cup frozen whole kernel corn
1 jar (16-ounces) salsa
1/2 cup water

Directions

Trim the fat from the meat and cut into 1-inch pieces. Sprinkle the meat with ancho chile pepper, tossing to coat all sides. Lightly coat a large skillet with nonstick cooking spray and heat over medium-high heat. Cook the meat half at a time in the hot skillet until browned.

Combine the frozen stew vegetables and frozen corn in a 3-1/2 to 4-quart slow cooker. Add the meat and pour the salsa and water over the mixture in the cooker.

Cover and cook on LOW for 8 to 9 hours or on HIGH for 4 to 4-1/2 hours.

Makes 4 servings.

Per Serving

Calories: 272; Fat: 5g; Cholesterol: 50mg; Sodium: 84mg; Carbohydrate: 28g; Fiber: 5g; Protein: 30g

Corned Beef and Cabbage

Plan this Irish classic for St. Paddy's Day or anytime you're in the mood for a bit o' green.

Preparation Time: 15 minutes
Cooking Time: 10 to 12 hours (LOW) or 5 to 6 hours (HIGH)

Ingredients

1 3-to-4 pound corned beef brisket with spice packet
1/2 of a small head cabbage, cut into 3 wedges
4 medium carrots, halved lengthwise and cut into 2-inch pieces
2 medium Yukon gold or yellow Finn potatoes, cut into 2-inch pieces
1 medium onion, quartered
1/2 cup water

Directions

Trim the fat from the corned beef brisket. If necessary, cut the meat to fit into a 5 to 6-quart slow cooker. Sprinkle the brisket evenly with the spice from the packet and rub the spice in with your fingers.

Place the cabbage, carrots, potatoes, and onion in the slow cooker and add water.

Place the brisket on top of the vegetables.

Cover and cook on LOW for 10 to 12 hours or on HIGH for 5 to 6 hours.

Transfer the meat to a serving platter and thinly slice the brisket against the grain. Using a slotted spoon, transfer the vegetables to the platter.

Makes 6 servings.

Per Serving

Calories: 457; Fat: 27g; Cholesterol: 115mg; Sodium: 1,543mg; Carbohydrate: 16g; Fiber: 3g; Protein: 35g

Easy Taco Chili Stew

Make dinner more fun by passing bowls of corn chips, sour cream, and sliced green onions to top off this Tex-Mex stew.

Preparation time: 15 minutes
Cooking time: 4 to 6 hours (LOW) or 2 to 3 hours (HIGH)

Ingredients

1 pound lean ground beef
2 cans (14-1/2 ounces, each) Mexican-style stewed tomatoes, undrained
1 can (15-1/4 ounces) whole kernel corn, undrained
1 can (15-ounces) red kidney beans, undrained
1 package (1-1/4 ounces) taco seasoning mix

Directions

Cook the ground beef in a large skillet over medium-high heat until browned while breaking up the meat with a wooden spoon.

Transfer the meat to a 3-1/2 to 4-quart slow cooker and stir in the tomatoes, corn, beans, and taco seasoning mix.

Cover and cook on LOW for 4 to 6 hours or on HIGH for 2 to 3 hours.

Makes 4 to 6 servings.

Per Serving

Calories: 464; Fat: 17g; Cholesterol: 71mg; Sodium: 2,317mg; Carbohydrate: 50g; Fiber: 9g; Protein: 33g

Italian-Style Meatballs with Basil Pesto Stew

This meatball stew will warm you from the inside regardless of how cold it may be outside.

Preparation time: 10 minutes
Cooking time: 5 to 7 hours (LOW) or 2-1/2 to 3-1/2 hours (HIGH)

Ingredients

2 cans (14-1/2 ounces, each) Italian style stewed tomatoes, undrained
1 package (16-ounces) frozen cooked Italian-style meatballs (about 32), thawed
1 can (15 to 19-ounces) cannellini (white kidney) beans, rinsed and drained
1/2 cup water
1/4 cup basil pesto
1/2 cup Parmesan cheese (2-ounces), finely shredded

Directions

Combine the tomatoes, meatballs, beans, water and pesto in a 3-1/2 to 4-quart slow cooker.

Cover and cook on LOW for 5 to 7 hours or HIGH for 2-1/2 to 3-1/2 hours.

Sprinkle the Parmesan cheese on each serving.

Makes 6 servings.

Per Serving

Calories: 408; Fat: 27g; Cholesterol: 34mg; Sodium: 1,201mg; Carbohydrate: 24g; Fiber: 6g; Protein: 17g

Perfect Pot Roast

Want a healthier roast? Cook, cover, and refrigerate overnight, then skim the fat off the top before reheating and serving.

Preparation time: 15 minutes
Cooking time: 8 hours (LOW) of 4 hours (HIGH)

Ingredients

4 to 5 pounds bottom round or rump roast
1 tablespoon olive or canola oil
2 cups beef broth
2 cups ketchup
1/2 cup cider vinegar
2 medium onions, chopped
2 cloves garlic, minced (optional)
6 tablespoons brown sugar
5 carrots, quartered
5 ribs celery

Directions

Rub the roast with oil and brown under a broiler on both sides.

In a 4-quart or larger slow cooker, combine the broth, ketchup, vinegar, onions, garlic, and the sugar.

Add the roast, carrots and celery.

Cover and cook on LOW for 8 hours or on HIGH for 4 hours.

Slice and serve with vegetables and sauce from the cooker.

Makes 12 servings.

Per Serving

Calories: 380; Fat: 11g; Cholesterol: 125mg; Sodium: 770mg; Carbohydrate: 28g; Fiber: 2g; Protein: 42g

Beef and Marinara Sauce Stuffed Peppers

Bell peppers pack more than 100% of your daily value of vitamins C and A.

Preparation time: 15 minutes
Cooking time: 8 hours (LOW) or 4 hours (HIGH)

Ingredients

1 jar (26-ounces) marinara sauce
1 tablespoons red wine vinegar
1 teaspoon ground cumin
1/4 teaspoon ground cinnamon
1/2 large bell pepper, finely chopped
4 large bell peppers, seeded with top removed and reserved
8 ounces lean ground beef
1/2 cup converted rice
1/3 cup finely chopped onion

Directions

Stir the sauce, vinegar, cumin and cinnamon in a medium bowl and pour 1-1/3 cups of the sauce mixture into a 3-1/2 to 4-quart slow cooker.

Combine the beef, rice, onion, chopped pepper, and the remaining sauce mixture in a large bowl. Spoon the mixture into the peppers and replace the tops. Place in the slow cooker.

Cover and cook on LOW for 8 hours or on HIGH for 4 hours, or until the filling is cooked through.

Serve with the sauce from the pot.

Makes 4 servings.

Per Serving

Calories: 360; Fat: 10g; Cholesterol: 20mg; Sodium: 810mg; Carbohydrate: 51g; Fiber: 7g; Protein: 18g

Swedish Meatballs with Ground Beef and Pork

Serve these easy to make Swedish meatballs with egg noodles and your choice of salad for a filling supper.

Preparation time: 15 minutes
Cooking time: 15 minutes (HIGH) plus 4 to 5 hours (LOW)

Ingredients

1-1/2 pounds lean ground beef
1 pound ground pork
1 cup onions, chopped fine
1-1/2 cups fine dried bread crumbs
2 tablespoons minced parsley
2 eggs, lightly beaten
1 cup fat-free milk
2 tablespoons Worcestershire sauce
Salt, to taste
1 teaspoon garlic powder
1/4 teaspoon black pepper
4 tablespoons canola oil

Directions

Shape the beef, pork, onions, bread crumbs, parsley, eggs, milk, Worcestershire, salt, garlic powder, and pepper into walnut-sized balls.

Brown in a skillet over medium heat and then place in several 4-quart slow cookers. Cover and cook on high for 15 minutes. Pour the gravy of your choice over the meatballs.

Cover and reduce heat to low and cook for 4 to 5 hours.

Makes 24 servings.

Per Serving

Calories: 200; Fat: 12g; Cholesterol: 50mg; Sodium: 360mg; Carbohydrate: 11g; Fiber: 0g; Protein: 11g

Chicken

THE RECIPES

Apricot Chicken 24
Chicken a la King 25
Chicken and Corn Chowder 26
Chicken Chili 27
Chicken Curry in a Hurry 28
Chicken Vegetables with Hoisin Sauce 30
Creamy Chicken Noodle with Mixed Vegetables Soup 32
Dill-Lemon Chicken 34
Easy Chicken Tostadas 35
Oriental Chicken 37
Santa Fe Chicken 38
Simple Chicken 39
Smoky Chicken-Potato Casserole 40
Sweet 'N' Sour Chicken 41

Apricot Chicken

Apricots are a health all-star; 1 cup of nectar packs 70% of your daily value for vitamin A/beta-carotene.

Preparation time: 15 minutes
Cooking time: 6 to 8 hours (LOW) or 3 to 4 hours (HIGH)

Ingredients

8 boneless chicken breasts or thighs, skin removed
1 package (2-ounces) onion soup mix
1 to 2 cans (12-ounces, each) apricot nectar
1 cup dried apricots

Directions

Put the chicken in a 3-1/2 to 4-quart slow cooker and sprinkle with the soup mix then cover with the nectar and apricots.

Cover and cook on LOW 6 to 8 hours or on HIGH for 3 to 4 hours, or until the chicken is thoroughly cooked.

Makes 8 servings.

Per Serving

Calories: 220; Fat: 3 g; Cholesterol: 70mg; Sodium: 130mg;
Carbohydrate: 19g; Fiber: 1g; Protein: 28g

Chicken a la King

Serve over brown rice instead of white for extra fiber and nutrients.

Preparation time: 15 minutes
Cooking time: 5 to 5-1/2 hours (LOW) or 2-1/2 to 3 hours (HIGH), plus 20 to 30 minutes (HIGH)

Ingredients

1-1/2 pounds boneless, skinless chicken breast, cut into bite-size pieces
1 can (10-3/4-ounces) fat-free, low sodium cream of chicken soup
3 tablespoons all-purpose flour
1/4 teaspoon black pepper
1 package (9-ounces) frozen peas and onions, thawed and drained
2 tablespoons chopped pimientos
1/2 teaspoon paprika

Directions

Place the chicken in a 3-1/2 to 4-quart slow cooker.

Combine the soup, flour and pepper and pour over the chicken. Do not stir.

Cover and cook on LOW for 5 to 5-1/2 hours or on HIGH for 2-1/2 to 3 hours.

Stir in the peas and onions, pimientos, and paprika and cover and cook on HIGH for an additional 20 to 30 minutes.

Makes 6 servings.

Per Serving

Calories: 280; Fat: 7g; Cholesterol: 100mg; Sodium: 510mg;
Carbohydrate: 13g; Fiber: 2g; Protein: 39g

Chicken and Corn Chowder

Stir the half-and-half into the colorful soup just before serving so it doesn't curdle.

Preparation time: 15 minutes
Cooking time: 4 to 6 hours (LOW) or 2 to 3 hours (HIGH)

Ingredients

1 pound skinless, boneless chicken thighs, cut into 1/2 to 3/4 inch pieces
2 cans (10-3/4-ounces, each) condensed cream of potato or cream of chicken soup
1-1/2 cups sliced celery (3 stalks)
1 can (11-ounces) whole kernel corn with sweet peppers, undrained
1 cup water
1 cup half-and-half or light cream

Directions

Combine the chicken, soup, celery, corn and the water in a 3-1/2 to 4-1/2-quart slow cooker.

Cover and cook on LOW for 4 to 6 hours or on HIGH for 2 to 3 hours. Stir in the half-and-half.

Makes 6 servings.

Per Serving

Calories: 261; Fat: 10g; Cholesterol: 86mg; Sodium: 1,029mg; Carbohydrate: 24g; Fiber: 3g; Protein: 19g

Chicken Chili

Chili beans, also known as kidney beans, are the ultimate health food. They're loaded with B vitamins, fiber, magnesium, and protein.

Preparation time: 15 minutes
Cooking time: 8 hours (LOW) or 4 hours (HIGH)

Ingredients

3 cups cooked and cubed chicken
1 large onion, chopped
3 cans (12-ounces, each) low-sodium chili beans, undrained
1 can (12-ounces) low-sodium chopped tomatoes, undrained
1 can (6-ounces) low-sodium tomato paste
1 cup frozen corn
3 tablespoons chili powder

Directions

Combine all the ingredients in a 3-1/2 to 4-quart slow cooker and stir well.

Cover and cook on LOW for 8 hours or on HIGH for 4 hours.

Makes 10 servings.

Per Serving

Calories: 250; Fat: 4g; Cholesterol: 60mg; Sodium: 560mg;
Carbohydrate: 26g; Fiber: 7g; Protein: 28g

Chicken Curry in a Hurry

Frozen stew vegetables eliminate peeling and chopping, keeping preparation time to a minimum.

Preparation time: 15 minutes
Cooking time: 6 to 7 hours (LOW) or 3 to 3-1/2 hours (HIGH)

Ingredients

1 package (16-ounces) frozen stew vegetables
4 large bone-in chicken thighs (1-1/2 to 1-3/4 pounds total), skinned
Salt
Ground black pepper
1 can (10-3/4-ounces) condensed cream of potato soup
2 teaspoons curry powder
1 tablespoon snipped fresh cilantro

Directions

Place the frozen vegetables in a 3-1/2 to 4-quart slow cooker and top with the chicken. Sprinkle with salt and pepper.

Stir together the soup and curry powder in a small bowl and pour over the chicken.

Cover and cook on LOW for 6 to 7 hours or on HIGH for 3 to 3-1/2 hours.

Remove the chicken from the slow cooker then strip and discard the bones. If desired, break the chicken into large pieces the return the chicken to the slow cooker and stir to combine.

Sprinkle each serving with cilantro.

Makes 6 servings.

Per Serving

Calories: 200; Fat: 5g; Cholesterol: 97mg; Sodium: 734mg; Carbohydrate: 13g; Fiber: 1g; Protein: 24g

Chicken Vegetables with Hoisin Sauce

Frozen stir fry vegetables provide a simple way to add lots of flavor, color, and vitamins to this dish.

Preparation time: 15 minutes
Cooking time: 4 to 5 hours (LOW) or 2-1/2 hours (HIGH), plus 30 minutes (HIGH)

Ingredients

Nonstick cooking spray
12 bone-in chicken thighs (3-1/2 to 4 pounds total), skinned
2 tablespoons quick-cooking tapioca
1/8 teaspoon ground black pepper
1/2 cup hoisin sauce
1 package (16-ounces) frozen stir-fry vegetables
3 cups hot cooked rice

Directions

Coat the inside of a 3-1/2 to 4-quart slow cooker with cooking spray.

Place the chicken in the prepared slow cooker and sprinkle with the tapioca, salt, and pepper then pour the hoisin sauce over the chicken.

Cover and cook on LOW for 4 to 5 hours or on HIGH for 2-1/2 hours.

If using the LOW setting, turn to HIGH and stir in the frozen vegetables. Cover and cook for an additional 30 to 45 minutes or just until the vegetables are tender.

Serve over the hot cooked rice.

Makes 6 servings.

Per Serving

Calories: 345; Fat: 6g; Cholesterol: 115mg; Sodium: 537mg; Carbohydrate: 37g; Fiber: 3g; Protein: 32g

Creamy Chicken Noodle with Mixed Vegetables Soup

Many folks say homemade chicken noodle soup helps battle a cold or the flu. Even doubters agree its comforting flavor has great appeal.

Preparation time: 15 minutes
Cooking time: Cook 6 to 8 hours (LOW) or 3 to 4 hours (HIGH), plus 20 minutes (HIGH)

Ingredients

5 cups water
2 cans (10-ounces, each) condensed cream of chicken and mushroom soup
2 cups cooked chicken (about 10-ounces), chopped
1 package (10-ounces) frozen mixed vegetables (cut green beans, corn, carrots, and peas)
1 teaspoon seasoned pepper or garlic pepper
1-1/2 cups dried egg noodles

Directions

Slowly stir the water into the chicken and mushroom soup in a 3-1/2 to 4-quart slow cooker until smooth.

Stir in the cooked chicken, frozen vegetables, and seasoned pepper.

Cover and cook on LOW for 6 to 8 hours or on HIGH for 3 to 4 hours.

If using LOW heat, turn to HIGH and stir in the uncooked dried egg noodles. Cover and cook for an additional 20 to 30 minutes (or until the noodles are tender).

Makes 6 to 8 servings.

Per Serving

Calories: 262; Fat: 12g; Cholesterol: 63mg; Sodium: 908mg; Carbohydrate: 21g; Fiber: 3g; Protein: 19g

Dill-Lemon Chicken

Swapping in fat-free sour cream for the real deal slashes the fat and calories, but preserves the creamy flavor.

Preparation time: 15 minutes
Cooking time: 3 to 4 hours on LOW

Ingredients

1 cup fat-free sour cream
1 tablespoon fresh dill, minced
1 teaspoon lemon-pepper seasoning
1 teaspoon lemon zest
4 boneless, skinless chicken breast halves

Directions

Combine the sour cream, dill, lemon-pepper, and lemon zest and spoon 1/4 of the mixture into a 3-1/2 to 4-quart slow cooker.

Arrange the chicken breasts on top of the mixture in a single layer.

Pour the remaining sauce over the chicken and spread evenly.

Cover and cook on LOW for 3 to 4 hours.

Makes 4 servings.

Per Serving

Calories: 200; Fat: 4g; Cholesterol: 80mg; Sodium: 230mg;
Carbohydrate: 10g; Fiber: 0g; Protein: 30g

Easy Chicken Tostadas

Buy a roasted chicken from the deli or use leftover cooked chicken for these tasty stacks.

Preparation time: 15 minutes
Cooking time: 5 to 6 hours (LOW) or 2-1/2 to 3 hours (HIGH)

Ingredients

4 cups cooked chicken, shredded
1 package (16-ounces) frozen onion and sweet peppers vegetable stir-fry mix
2 cups (about 8-ounces) shredded Mexican cheese blend
12 tostada shells
2 cans (10-ounces, each) enchilada sauce
1-1/2 cups fresh spinach leaves, shredded (optional)
Sour cream (optional)

Directions

Combine the chicken, frozen vegetables, and Mexican cheese in a 4 to 5-quart slow cooker.

Coarsely break six of the tostada shell and reserve the remaining six shells until ready to serve. Add the broken tostada shells to the mixture in the slow cooker.

Stir in the enchilada sauce.

Cover and cook on LOW for 5 to 6 hours or on HIGH for 2-1/2 to 3 hours.

To serve, take the chicken mixture and divide it among the reserved six tostada shells. You may top with spinach and/or sour cream.

Makes 6 servings.

Per Serving

Calories: 409; Fat: 26g; Cholesterol: 100mg; Sodium: 1,427mg; Carbohydrate: 20g; Fiber: 3g; Protein: 25g

Oriental Chicken

Serve with steamed bok choy or broccoli; these cruciferous veggies have potent anticancer properties.

Preparation time: 15 minutes
Cooking time: 4 to 6 hours (LOW) or 2 to 3 hours (HIGH)

Ingredients

1/2 cup light soy sauce
1/2 cup honey
2 tablespoons sesame seeds (optional)
6 boneless, skinless chicken breast halves

Directions

Mix the soy sauce, honey and sesame seeds (if using).

Place the chicken in a 3-1/2 to 4-quart slow cooker, spooning 2 tablespoons of the soy-honey mixture over each breast. Pour any of the remaining sauce over the top after all the chicken is in the cooker.

Cover and cook on LOW for 4 to 6 hours or on HIGH for 2 to 3 hours.

Makes 6 servings.

Per Serving

Calories: 170; Fat: 2g; Cholesterol: 35mg; Sodium: 740mg;
Carbohydrate: 25g; Fiber: 0g; Protein: 15g

Santa Fe Chicken

Choose jarred salsa with exotic ingredients like mango, fire-roasted peppers, or garlic for extra zing - without the effort.

Preparation time: 15 minutes
Cooking time: 5 to 7 hours on LOW or 3 hours on HIGH

Ingredients

2 cans (15-ounces, each) Mexican corn with red and green peppers
1 can (16-ounces) pink beans
1 cup low-sodium chicken broth
1 cup chunky-style salsa
6 boneless, skinless chicken breast halves, sliced into 1-inch strips

Directions

Put the corn, beans, chicken broth, salsa, and the chicken in a 3-1/2 to 4-quart slow cooker and stir to combine.

Cover and cook on LOW for 5 to 7 hours or on HIGH for about 3 hours, or until the chicken is tender.

Makes 6 servings.

Per Serving

Calories: 330; Fat: 2g; Cholesterol: 70mg; Sodium: 1,320mg; Carbohydrate: 37g; Fiber: 7g; Protein: 34g

Simple Chicken

Serve this high-protein, low-carb dish on a bed of steamed baby spinach to add iron and folate to your meal.

Preparation time: 15 minutes
Cooking time: 8 to 1o hours (LOW) or 4 to 5 hours (HIGH)

Ingredients

4 boneless, skinless chicken breast halves
1 package dry Italian dressing mix
1 cup warm water or chicken broth

Directions

Place the chicken in a 3-1/2 to 4-quart slow cooker and sprinkle with the Italian dressing mix.

Pour the water over the chicken.

Cover and cook on LOW for 8 to 10 hours or on HIGH on 4 to 5 hours.

Makes 6 servings.

Per Serving

Calories: 160; Fat: 3g; Cholesterol: 75mg; Sodium: 650mg; Carbohydrate: 6g; Fiber: 0g; Protein: 27g

Smoky Chicken-Potato Casserole

Smoked chicken and cheese give this creamy comfort food impressive flavor. Because this recipe contains sour cream and cheese, use only the low-heat setting to cook it.

Preparation time: 15 minutes
Cooking time: 5 to 6 hours (LOW)

Ingredients

Nonstick cooking spray
1 can (10-3/4-ounces) condensed cream of chicken with herbs soup
1-1/2 cups shredded smoked cheddar cheese (about 6-ounces)
1 carton (8-ounces) sour cream
1 package (28-ounces) frozen diced hash brown potatoes with onions and peppers, thawed
3 cups chopped smoked or roasted chicken or turkey (about 1 pound)
Crushed croutons (optional)

Directions

Lightly coat the inside of a 3-1/2 to 4-quart slow cooked with the cooking spray.

Combine the soup, cheese and the sour cream in the prepared slow cooker and then stir in the potatoes and chicken.

Cover and cook on LOW for 5 to 6 hours.

If desired, top each serving with croutons.

Makes 6 servings.

Per Serving

Calories: 399; Fat: 20g; Cholesterol: 80mg; Sodium: 1,313mg; Carbohydrate: 31g; Fiber: 3g; Protein: 25g

Sweet 'N' Sour Chicken

Preparing this simple dinner may be even less hassle than ordering takeout. To round out the meal, bake frozen egg roll appetizers and serve fortune cookies and sherbet for dessert.

Preparation time: 15 minutes
Cooking time: 5 to 5-1/2 hours (LOW) or 2-1/2 to 2-3/4 hours (HIGH)

Ingredients

1 pound skinless, boneless chicken breast
2 jars (9 or 10-ounces, each) sweet-and-sour sauce
1 package (16-ounces) frozen broccoli, carrots and water chestnuts
2-1/2 cups hot cooked rice
1/4 cup chopped almonds, toasted

Directions

Cut the chicken into 1-inch pieces.

Combine the chicken, sweet-and-sour sauce, and frozen vegetables in a 3-1/2 to 4-quart slow cooker.

Cover and cook on LOW for 5 to 5-1/2 hours or on HIGH for 2-1/2 to 2-3/4 hours.

Serve with hot cooked rice and sprinkle with almonds.

Makes 4 servings.

Per Serving

Calories: 477; Fat: 6g; Cholesterol: 66mg; Sodium: 418mg;
Carbohydrate: 71g; Fiber: 4g; Protein: 32g

Fish

THE RECIPES

Tuna Casserole 43
Tuna with White Beans 44

Tuna Casserole

This classic comfort food is a tasty, convenient way to get heart-healthy Omega-3 fats into your family's diet.

Preparation time: 15 minutes
Cooking time: 4 to 6 hours (LOW) or 2 to 3 hours (HIGH)

Ingredients

2 cans (16-ounces, each) tuna, packed in water
1-1/2 cups cooked macaroni
1/2 cup onions, finely chopped
1/4 cup green bell peppers, finely chopped
4 ounces sliced mushrooms, drained
10 ounce bag frozen cauliflower, partially thawed
1/2 cup sodium and fat-free chicken broth

Directions

Combine all the ingredients in a 3-1/2 to 4-quart slow cooker and stir well.

Cover and cook on LOW for 4 to 6 hours or on HIGH for 2 to 3 hours.

Makes 6 servings.

Per Serving

Calories: 210; Fat: 3g; Cholesterol: 35mg; Sodium: 1,940mg; Carbohydrate: 16g; Fiber: 3g; Protein: 32g

Tuna with White Beans

One cup of white beans packs two-thirds of your daily fiber needs, and tuna is a good source of protein and healthy fats.

Preparation time: 15 minutes
Cooking time: 5 to 7 hours (LOW) or 2-1/2 to 3-1/2 hours (HIGH), plus 30 minutes (HIGH)

Ingredients

2 cups tomato-based pasta sauce
1 can (16-ounces) white beans, rinsed and drained
2 cans (12-ounces, each) solid white tuna, drained and flaked
Salt and freshly ground black pepper, to taste

Directions

Put the pasta sauce and white beans in a 4-quart or larger slow cooker and stir to combine.

Cover and cook on LOW for 5 to 7 hours or on HIGH for 2-1/2 to 3-1/2 hours.

Add the flaked tuna and stir with the ingredients already in the slow cooker. Cover and cook on HIGH for an additional 30 minutes.

Before serving, stir the mixture again and season with the salt and pepper to taste.

Serve with rice, pasta or bread.

Makes 8 servings.

Per Serving

Calories: 200; Fat: 5g; Cholesterol: 30mg; Sodium: 560mg; Carbohydrate: 15g; Fiber: 4g; Protein: 21g

Pork

THE RECIPES

Ham, Cheese and Potato Soup 46
Apricot-Glazed Pork Roast 47
Old Fashion Black Bean Soup 48
Bratwursts and Beer 50
Country-Style Pork Ribs with Cranberry and Chipotle 52
Ham with Potato au Gratin 54
Hominy-Pork Stew 55

Ham, Cheese and Potato Soup

This rich, creamy soup - without the fat and calories - can be garnished with red pepper strips for an extra shot of vitamin C and fiber.

Preparation time: 15 minutes
Cooking time: 4 hours (HIGH)

Ingredients

3 cups of water
1 cup diced ham
5 medium potatoes, diced fine
1 package (8-ounces) fat-free cream cheese, cubed
1/2 medium onion, chopped
1 teaspoon garlic salt
1/2 teaspoon black pepper
1/2 teaspoon dill weed

Directions

Combine all the ingredients in a 3-1/2 to 4-quart slow-cooker.

Cover and cook on HIGH for 4 hours, stirring occasionally.

Turn to low until ready to serve.

Makes 6 servings.

Per Serving

Calories: 220; Fat: 3g; Cholesterol: 25mg; Sodium: 400mg;
Carbohydrate: 34g; Fiber: 4g; Protein: 16g

Apricot-Glazed Pork Roast

Preparation time: 15 minutes
Cooking time: 10 to 12 hours (LOW) or 5 to 6 hours (HIGH)

Ingredients

1 3 to 3-1/2 pound boneless pork shoulder roast
1 jar (18-ounces) apricot preserves
1 cup chopped onion (about 1 large)
1/4 cup chicken broth
2 tablespoons Dijon-style mustard
3 to 4 cups hot cooked rice (optional)

Directions

Trim the fat from the boneless pork shoulder roast. If necessary, cut the pork shoulder roast to fit into a 3-1/2 to 6-quart slow cooker, then place the meat in the slow cooker.

For the sauce, combine the apricot preserves, onion, chicken broth, and the mustard in a small bowl and then pour over the pork meat.

Cover and cook on LOW for 10 to 12 hours or on HIGH for 5 to 6 hours.

Transfer the meat to a serving platter. Skim the fat from the sauce and spoon some of the sauce over the meat.

Serve with hot cooked rice (if desired) mixed into the remaining sauce.

Makes 6 to 8 servings.

Per Serving

Calories: 456; Fat: 10g; Cholesterol: 93mg; Sodium: 184mg;
Carbohydrate: 61g; Fiber: 2g; Protein: 29g

Old Fashion Black Bean Soup

Black beans are an off-the-charts source of fiber and antioxidants.

Preparation time: 15 minutes
Cooking time: 1 hours (HIGH) plus 7 hours (LOW)

Ingredients

1 can (16-ounces) black beans
1 ham bone or ham hock
6 cups chicken broth or water
2 tablespoons butter
2 medium onions, chopped
2 cloves garlic, minced
1 cup chopped celery
1 teaspoon dried marjoram
1 bay leaf

Directions

Combine the drained beans, ham, and broth in a 3-1/2 to 4-quart slow cooker.

Cover and cook on HIGH for about 1 hour.

Meanwhile, sauté the onions, garlic, and celery in butter in a large skillet over medium heat for about 5 minutes. Add to the slow cooker with the marjoram and bay leaf.

Cover and turn the cooker to LOW and cook for 7 hours.

Discard the bay leaf and ham bone or hock and purée with a hand-held immersion blender.

Makes 6 servings.

Per Serving

Calories: 420; Fat: 7g; Cholesterol: 10mg; Sodium: 940mg; Carbohydrate: 74g; Fiber: 18g; Protein: 20g

Bratwursts and Beer

Don't know what to bring to your next tailgate party? Simply double this simple, people-pleasing recipe and impress your friends.

Preparation time: 15 minutes
Cooking time: 4 to 5 hours (LOW) or 2 to 2-1/2 hours (HIGH)

Ingredients

8 bratwursts
1 large onion, sliced
1 can (12-ounces) beer
1 cup bottled chili sauce
1 cup ketchup
2 tablespoons vinegar
1 tablespoon Worcestershire sauce
2 tablespoons brown sugar
1 tablespoon paprika
1/2 teaspoon salt

Directions

Place the bratwursts in a water filled skillet and boil for 10 minutes to remove the fat.

Drain the bratwursts and place in a 4-quart or large slow cooker.

Mix together the remaining ingredients in a large bowl and pour over the meat.

Cover and cook on LOW for 4 to 5 hours or HIGH for 2 to 2-1/2 hours.

Makes 8 servings.

Per Serving

Calories: 160; Fat: 5g; Cholesterol: 10mg; Sodium: 1,000mg; Carbohydrate: 24g; Fiber: 1g; Protein: 3g

Country-Style Pork Ribs with Cranberry and Chipotle

Country style ribs are cut from the end of the pork loin, next to the shoulder. They have a slightly higher fat content and more meat than spare or back ribs, so they are a perfect cut for long, slow cooking.

Preparation time: 15 minutes
Cooking time: 7 to 8 hours (LOW) or 3-1/2 to 4 hours (HIGH)

Ingredients

2-1/2 to 3 pounds of country style boneless pork ribs
Salt
Ground black pepper
1 can (16-ounces) whole cranberry sauce
1 cup onion (about 1 large), chopped
3 chipotle peppers in adobo sauce, finely chopped
1-1/2 teaspoons of minced garlic (about 3 cloves)

Directions

Trim the fat from the boneless pork ribs and sprinkle the ribs with salt and black pepper. Place the ribs in a 3 1/2 or 4-quart slow cooker.

For the sauce, combine the cranberry sauce, onion, chipotle peppers, and garlic in a medium bowl.

Pour the sauce over the ribs.

Cover and cook on LOW for 7 to 8 hours or on HIGH for 3-1/2 to 4 hours.

Transfer the ribs to a serving plate.

Stir the sauce and drizzle over the ribs.

Makes 6 to 8 servings.

Per Serving

Calories: 395; Fat: 10g; Cholesterol: 139mg; Sodium: 247mg;
Carbohydrate: 32g; Fiber: 2g; Protein: 40g

Ham with Potato au Gratin

Preparation time: 15 minutes
Cooking time: 7 to 8 hours on LOW or 3-1/2 to 4 hours on HIGH

Ingredients

Nonstick cooking spray
2 cups of cubed cooked ham (about 10-ounces)
2 packages (4.9-ounces) dry au gratin potato mix
1/4 cup roasted red sweet pepper, chopped and drained
3 cups water
1 can (10-3/4-ounces) condensed cheddar cheese soup
Fresh snipped chives (optional)

Directions

Take the nonstick cooking spray and lightly coat the inside of a 3-1/2 or 4-quart slow cooker.

Combine the cubed cooked ham, packages of dry au gratin potato mix and the roasted red sweet pepper in the prepared cooker.

In a medium sized bowl, gradually stir the water into the cheddar cheese soup then pour over the mixture in the slow cooker.

Cover and cook on LOW for 7 to 8 hours or on HIGH for 3-1/2 to 4 hours.

You may garnish each serving with fresh chives.

Makes 6 servings.

Per Serving

Calories: 255; Fat: 7g; Cholesterol: 29mg; Sodium: 2,087mg; Carbohydrate: 45g; Fiber: 3g; Protein: 15g

Hominy-Pork Stew

Preparation time: 15 minutes
Cooking time: 8 to 9 hours (LOW) or 4 to 4-1/2 hours (HIGH)

Ingredients

2 pounds boneless pork shoulder roast
1-1/2 teaspoons ground cumin
Nonstick cooking spray
Disposable slow cooker liner
1 can (15-1/2-ounces) hominy, rinsed and drained
1 can (15-ounces) navy beans, rinsed and drained
1 jar (16-ounces) tequila-lime salsa
1-1/4 cups water
Lime wedges (optional)

Directions

Trim the fat from the pork shoulder roast and cut the meat into 1-inch pieces.

Place the pork shoulder roast in a medium bowl and sprinkle the meat with cumin, tossing to coat on all sides.

Lightly coat a large skillet with the cooking spray and heat the skillet over medium-high heat. Cook the pork shoulder roast, half at a time, in the hot skillet until browned.

Combine the meat, hominy, and beans in a 3-1/2 or 4-quart slow cooker then stir in the salsa and the water.

Cover and cook on LOW for 8 to 9 hours or on HIGH for 4 to 4-1/2 hours.

If desired, serve with the lime wedges.

Makes 4 servings.

Per Serving

Calories: 527; Fat: 16g; Cholesterol: 151mg; Sodium: 1,186mg; Carbohydrate: 41g; Fiber: 8g; Protein: 52g

Turkey

THE RECIPES

Mexican Style Turkey Meatball Stew 58
Turkey Breast with Orange Sauce 59
Turkey Meat Loaf 60

Mexican Style Turkey Meatball Stew

Meatballs hail from Italy, but this spicy sauce is definitely Mexican. Together the pair make a hearty and comforting supper.

Preparation time: 10 minutes
Cooing time: 6 to 7 hours (low) or 3 to 3-1/2 hours (high)

Ingredients

2 cans (14-1/2-ounces, each) Mexican-style stewed tomatoes, undrained
2 packages (12-ounces, each) frozen cooked Italian-style turkey meatballs (24 in total), thawed
1 can (15-ounces) black beans, rinsed and drained
1 can (14-ounces) seasoned chicken broth with roasted garlic
1 package (10-ounces) frozen whole kernel corn, thawed
Fresh oregano (optional)

Directions

Combine the tomatoes, meatballs, beans, broth and corn in a 4 to 5-quart slow cooker.

Cover and cook on LOW for 6 to 7 hours or on HIGH for 3 to 3-1/2 hours.

You may garnish each serving with oregano.

Makes 8 to 10 servings

Per Serving

Calories: 287; Fat: 13g; Cholesterol: 37mg; Sodium: 1,134mg; Carbohydrate: 30g; Fiber: 6g; Protein: 16g

Turkey Breast with Orange Sauce

One cup of orange juice has as much heart-healthy potassium as a banana, plus orange is a great source of vitamin C.

Preparation time: 15 minutes
Cooking time: 7 to 8 hours (LOW) or 3-1/2 to 4 hours (HIGH)

Ingredients

1 large onion, chopped
3 cloves garlic, minced
1 teaspoon dried rosemary
1/2 teaspoon black pepper
2 pounds boneless, skinless turkey breast
1-1/2 cup orange juice

Directions

Place the onion in a 4-quart or larger slow cooker.

Combine the garlic, rosemary, and pepper in a small bowl.

Make gashes in the turkey and stuff with the herb mixture.

Place the turkey in the slow cooker and pour the orange juice over the turkey.

Cover and cook on LOW for 7 to 8 hours or on HIGH 3-1/2 to 4 hours, or until the turkey is no longer pink in the center.

Slice and serve with the sauce.

Makes 6 servings.

Per Serving

Calories: 310; Fat: 2g; Cholesterol: 140mg; Sodium: 115mg;
Carbohydrate: 15g; Fiber: 0g; Protein: 57g

Turkey Meat Loaf

This lightened-up meat loaf really does taste better than mom's, but swapping lean turkey for beef cuts fat in half and slashes 130 calories.

Preparation time: 15 minutes
Cooking time: 6 to 8 hours (LOW) or 3 to 4 hours (HIGH)

Ingredients

1-1/2 pounds lean ground turkey
2 egg whites
1/3 cup ketchup
1 tablespoon Worcestershire sauce
1 teaspoon dried basil
1/2 teaspoon black pepper
2 small onions, chopped
2 medium potatoes, finely chopped
2 small red bell peppers, finely chopped

Directions

Combine all the ingredients in a large bowl.

Shape the loaf to fit in a 3-1/2 to 4-quart slow cooker and place in the cooker.

Cover and cook on LOW for 6 to 8 hours or on HIGH for 3 to 4 hours.

Makes 8 servings.

Per Serving

Calories: 200; Fat: 7g; Cholesterol: 65mg; Sodium: 380mg;
Carbohydrate: 16g; Fiber: 2g; Protein: 17g

Vegetarian

THE RECIPES

BBQ Veggie Joes	62
Cha-Cha Corn Chowder	63
Parmesan Risotto	64
Pasta Marinara	65
Potatoes au Gratin	67

BBQ Veggie Joes

A cup of cooked lentils provides 63% of your daily fiber needs, 37% of your iron, and packs 16 grams of protein.

Preparation time: 15 minutes
Cooking time: 8 to 10 hours (LOW) or 4 to 5 hours (HIGH)

Ingredients

1 cup dried lentils, picked over and rinsed
2 cups water
1-1/2 cups chopped celery
1-1/2 cups chopped carrots
1 cup chopped onions
3/4 cup ketchup
2 tablespoons brown sugar
2 tablespoons Worcestershire sauce
2 tablespoons cider vinegar

Directions

Combine the lentils and water in a medium saucepan, bring to a boil and then reduce the heat to low. Cover and let simmer for 10 minutes.

Combine the celery, carrots, onions, ketchup, sugar, Worcestershire, and lentils with water in a 4-quart or larger slow cooker. Mix well.

Cover and cook on LOW for 8 to 10 hours or on HIGH for 4 to 5 hours, or until the lentils are soft.

Stir in the vinegar before serving in pita bread or on rolls.

Makes 10 servings.

Per Serving

Calories: 230; Fat: 3g; Cholesterol: 0mg; Sodium: 480mg; Carbohydrate: 45g; Fiber: 9g; Protein: 10g

Cha-Cha Corn Chowder

Two kinds of corn give this soup a rich consistency and well balanced texture.

Preparation time: 15 minutes
Cooking time: 6 to 8 hours (LOW) or 3 to 4 hours (HIGH)

Ingredients

3 medium round red potatoes (about 1 pound), finely chopped
2 cans (14-3/4-ounces, each) cream-style corn
1 can (14-ounces) vegetable broth
1 can (11-ounces) whole kernel corn with sweet peppers, drained
1 can (4-ounces) diced green chile peppers, undrained
1/4 teaspoon ground black pepper
Cracked black pepper (optional)
Saltine crackers (optional)

Directions

Combine the potatoes, cream-style corn, broth, drained corn with peppers, undrained green chile peppers, and ground black pepper in a 3-1/2 or 4-quart slow cooker.

Cover and cook on LOW for 6 to 8 hours or on HIGH for 3 to 4 hours.

If desired, top each serving with cracked black pepper and/or serve with crackers.

Makes 6 servings.

Per Serving

Calories: 202; Fat: 1g; Cholesterol: 1mg; Sodium: 898mg; Carbohydrate: 49g; Fiber: 5g; Protein: 5g

Parmesan Risotto

Give risotto your own flair by adding your favorite veggies 2 hours before serving.

Preparation time: 15 minutes
Cooking time: 2 hours (HIGH)

Ingredients

1/4 cup olive oil
2 medium shallots, minced
1/4 cup dry white wine
1-1/4 cups arborio rice
3-3/4 cups vegetable broth
1/2 teaspoon salt
3/4 cup freshly grated Parmesan cheese

Directions

Warm the oil in a small skillet over medium heat. Cook the shallots until softened for approximately 3 to 4 minutes. Add the wine and cook, stirring, for a minute or so. Add the rice and cook, stirring, until it turns opaque, about 2 minutes.

Transfer into a 3-1/2 to 4-quart slow cooker with the broth and salt.

Cover and cook on HIGH for about 2 hours.

Stir in 1/2 cup of cheese and reserve the remainder for sprinkling.

Serve immediately.

Makes 6 servings.

Per Serving

Calories: 621; Fat: 4g; Cholesterol: 61mg; Sodium: 1,146mg; Carbohydrate: 80g; Fiber: 2g; Protein: 21g

Pasta Marinara

This sauce is rich in lycopene, a cancer-fighting antioxidant that gets more potent the longer it's cooked.

Preparation time: 15 minutes
Cooking time: 4 to 5 hours (LOW) or 2 to 2-1/2 hours (HIGH)

Ingredients

1/3 cup olive oil
1 medium yellow onion, finely chopped
1 clove garlic, minced
2 cans (28-ounces, each) whole plum tomatoes
3 ounces tomato paste
Salt and freshly ground black pepper, to taste

Directions

In medium skillet over medium heat, heat 3 tablespoons of oil and then cook the onion and garlic, stirring, until softened, about 5 minutes.

Transfer to a 4-quart or large slow cooker and add the remaining oil, tomatoes, and tomato paste. Stir to combine.

Cover and cook on LOW for 4 to 5 hours or on HIGH for 2 to 2-1/2 hours.

Season the sauce with salt and pepper to taste.

Use an immersion blender to purée the sauce in the insert.

Serve the sauce with hot pasta.

Makes 10 servings.

Per Serving

Calories: 100; Fat: 7g; Cholesterol: 0mg; Sodium: 270mg; Carbohydrate: 9g; Fiber: 2g; Protein: 2g

Potatoes au Gratin

Keep the skins on your potatoes and get 20% of your daily value of potassium and 40% of your Vitamin C requirements.

Preparation time: 15 minutes
Cooking time: 7 to 9 hours (LOW)

Ingredients

2 cans (10-3/4-ounces, each) condensed cheddar cheese soup
1 can (13-ounces) evaporated milk
1 bag (32-ounces) frozen oven chips or hash brown potatoes, partially thawed
Salt and freshly ground pepper, to taste

Directions

Coat the inside of a 4-quart or larger slow cooker with cooking spray.

Pour in the soup and milk and stir to combine.

Add the hash brown potatoes and stir again.

Cover and cook on LOW for 7 to 9 hours.

Before serving, stir the mixture and season with salt and pepper to taste.

Makes 10 servings.

Per Serving

Calories: 186; Fat: 8g; Cholesterol: 40mg; Sodium: 560mg;
Carbohydrate: 24g; Fiber: 2g; Protein: 7g

Conclusion

As you have seen in this cookbook, when it comes to creating quick and easy meals in a slow-cooker, the possibilities are endless. I encourage you to experiment and let you creative forces and imagination run wild and modify these recipes to your liking.

I sincerely hope that I have done a good job in introducing you to some of my favorite quick prep slow-cooker recipes and that I have provided valuable information that will help you in preparing your own fantastic slow-cooker meals.

You may also enjoy my other books:

- Vegetarian Slow Cooker Recipe Book: 30 Easy Set It & Forget It Meals
- Pressure Cooker Recipe Book: Fast Cooking Under Extreme Pressure
- Slow Cooker International Cooking: A Culinary Journey of Set It & Forget It Meals
- Vegetarian Slow Cooker Recipes: Top 71 Quick & Easy Vegetarian Crockpot Recipe Book
- Vegetarian Pressure Cooker Recipe Book: 50 High Pressure Recipes for Busy People
- 4 Ingredients or Less Cookbook: Fast, Practical & Healthy Meal Options
- Gluten-Free Diet Cookbook: Healthier Eating Choices for People with Celiac Disease
- Satisfying Slow Cooker Meals and More

For more information about myself and to enjoy more amazing recipes, please follow these links:

- Maria Holmes author page at www.amazon.com
- www.holmescookedmeals.com
- Holmes Cooked Meals Facebook page

I will be writing and publishing more cookbooks in the future, so please stay tuned. But for now, I would like to thank you for helping me and supporting my efforts to share my passion for cooking.

Thank you!

Index

Apricot Chicken 24
Apricot-Glazed Pork Roast 47
BBQ Veggie Joes 62
Beef and Marinara Sauce Stuffed Peppers 19
Beef with Ancho Chile Stew 12
Bratwursts and Beer 50
Cha-Cha Corn Chowder 63
Chicken a la King 25
Chicken and Corn Chowder 26
Chicken Chili 27
Chicken Curry in a Hurry 28
Chicken Vegetables with Hoisin Sauce 30
Corned Beef and Cabbage 13
Country-Style Pork Ribs with Cranberry and Chipotle 52
Creamy Chicken Noodle with Mixed Vegetables Soup 32
Dill-Lemon Chicken 34
Easy Chicken Tostadas 35
Easy Taco Chili Stew 15
Ham with Potato au Gratin 54
Ham, Cheese and Potato Soup 46
Hominy-Pork Stew 55
Italian-Style Meatballs with Basil Pesto Stew 16
Mexican Style Turkey Meatball Stew 58
Old Fashion Black Bean Soup 48
Oriental Chicken 37
Parmesan Risotto 64
Pasta Marinara 65
Perfect Pot Roast 17
Potatoes au Gratin 67
Roast Beef Sandwich 11
Roast Beef with Mixed Fruit and Chipotle Sauce 9
Santa Fe Chicken 38
Simple Chicken 39
Smoky Chicken-Potato Casserole 40
Swedish Meatballs with Ground Beef and Pork 21
Sweet 'N' Sour Chicken 41

Tuna Casserole 43
Tuna with White Beans 44
Turkey Breast with Orange Sauce 59
Turkey Meat Loaf 60

Printed in Great Britain
by Amazon